The Choir Director's Handbook?

by Charles Montgomery

© Copyright 1984 by LIGHT HEADED MUSIC PUBLISHING COMPANY
A Division of Light Hearted Music Publishing Company
P. O. Box 150246 - - Nashville, Tennessee 37215
Telephone 615 - 776-5678

1984 - 3.95

WISE OR OTHERWISE

At the lower portion of this page, you will find something that may resemble a coupon. If you feel absolutely led to write to the publisher concerning anything in this book, feel free to do so. On the opposite side of this portion, you will find the complete address of the publisher. This can be removed by a simple quick jerk. This may create problems for some of you, because in many or most churches you can find many simple jerks, but few of them are quick. But, that is your problem. Keep criticism at an absolute minimum. Put complaints in the box below. Be concise.

ALWAYS READ THE FINE PRINT

In case some of our readers wonder at the use, or mis-use of some of our great hymns in a frivolous way, I hasten to say, this was not done to take away from them. This has been done in fun and to encourage us to laugh at ourselves. I believe the God we worship is one who has a great sense of humor. When I see some of his strange creations, like a zebra, (I named mine 'Spot') the giraffe, or the duck-billed platypus, I know this has to be so. He even had to chuckle at some of us. So, I think He will like my book.

Charles Montgomery

(This is similar to a dotted line)

COMPLAINT BOX ☐
(Give full details)

Table of Contents

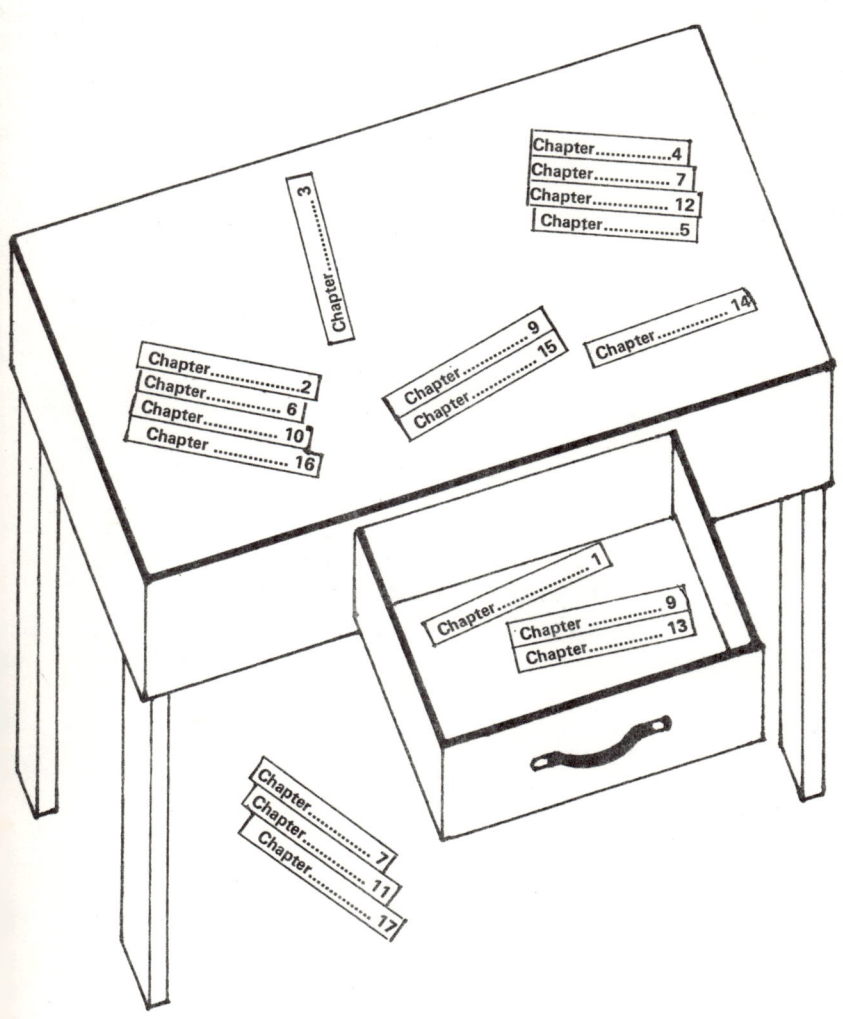

Dedication

This Handbook is respectfully dedicated
To *ALL* Choir Directors, Chorus Directors
or Ministers of Music,
Some of Whom were my Friends, but
Most of Whom I do not even Know—
May this book make your journey
A little easier along the way.

Charles Montgomery, AKA
O'MIAKIN BACH, Author of
RESTING

Foreword.....

Never having been a Choir Director or Chorus Director, I have long felt the need for Choir Directors to have a handbook that will give them directions in their directing. I have known that they need all the help they can get.

Having been a choir member for more years than I care to admit, and being out of a choir for some several years, I feel greatly qualified or dis-qualified, (depending on how you look at it) to write this handbook.

So, without any further ado, we shall get right into this handbook, which will be, in most cases, self-explanatory. If there are passages that are not quite clear to the reader, do not hesitate to write to the publisher for further enlightenment.

CHAPTER ONE

CHAPTER TWO

You will have noticed by now, we have omitted Chapter One. The reason for this, is, we just couldn't seem to get started on it. If you have not noticed this, please re-read Chapter One.

In this chapter, which is Chapter Two, we shall deal primarily with Part-time Choir Directors. Actually, we do not have a great deal of respect for Part-time Choir Directors, because if they are not willing to get in and suffer completely, there is not much we can do for them.

However, we shall try. I might add here, that the Part-time Director might just like to read Chapter Three only half-way through. It is devoted to Full-time Choir Directors. In defining Part-time Directors, we could say they use a lot of half-notes, perhaps only have half a choir, receive a half salary or less, and some have even said they are half-witted. Never-the-less, they need music, and the following page contains music that should be helpful.

MUSIC FOR PART-TIME CHOIR DIRECTORS
Purer in

FANNIE E. DAVIDSON

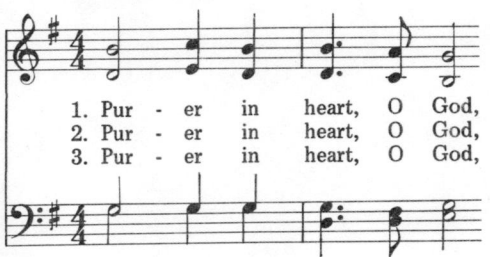

1. Pur - er in heart, O God,
2. Pur - er in heart, O God,
3. Pur - er in heart, O God,

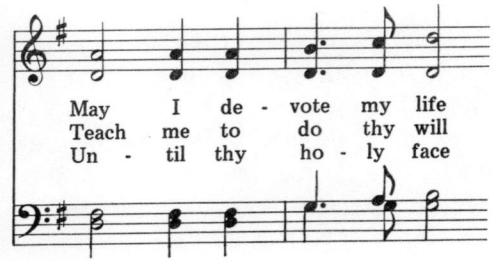

May I de - vote my life
Teach me to do thy will
Un - til thy ho - ly face

Watch thou my way - ward feet,
Be thou my friend and guide,
Keep me from se - cret sin,

Pur - er in heart Help
Pur - er in heart Help
Pur - er in heart Help

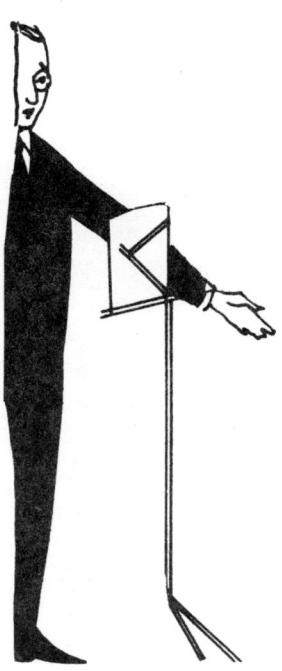

PICTURE OF PART-TIME CHOIR DIRECTOR

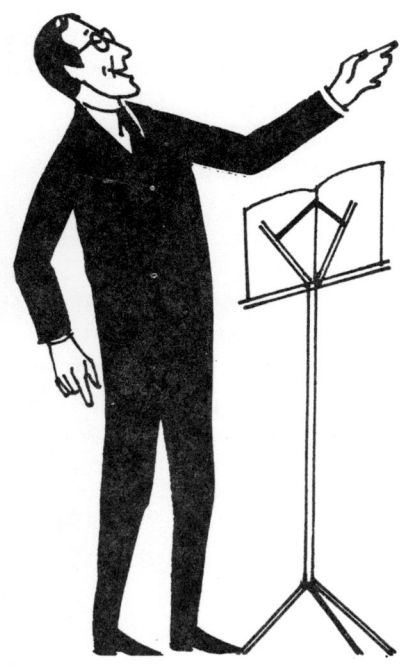

PICTURE OF FULL-TIME CHOIR DIRECTOR

CHAPTER THREE

In Chapter Three, we will be dealing with the Full-time Choir Director. You can feed the information given in Chapter Two into a computer and simply multiply by two (2) or even more, and this will give you an adequate description. If you do not have a computer available, this may complicate things. However, do the best you can.

CHAPTER FOUR

In Chapter Four, we will continue dealing with the Full-time Choir Director. One of his primary duties, (we use his here, since most are men, and we continue to believe his is sufficient to describe the unknown gender) is to lead the congregation. You can use your arm, or arms in directing. (Using both arms somewhat limits you to one song you may memorize, or if you wave the book in one hand, the front row occupants may be in some danger.) Or, if you want to really put on a show, use a baton. We might add here, that one of the advocates of baton was General Douglas McArthur in WW Two. He coined a phrase, "Back to Baton" which may have no meaning to some of the younger Directors. However, you can decide on which way you prefer to direct.

At this point, you certainly need to be reminded to develop some sort of cooperation with your pastor or minister. It need not be a great deal, because in all probability, he will not know the difference in any of your selections. But, it does seem to impress them if you tie in the Hymns with the Sermons. A few suggestions follows:

Sermon during Fire Prevention Week
It Only Takes a Spark to Get a Fire Going

Sermon on Marriages
Fight the Good Fight

Sermon During the Olympics
From Every Race, From Every Clime

Sermon, "It's Hard to Soar with Eagles,
          When You Work with a Bunch of Turkeys"
Have No Fear Little Flock

If Pastor closes sermon with old joke,
 I've Heard an Old, Old Story

If Preacher extends invitation and asks for another song,
 I Must Needs Go Home

   This will give you an idea how helpful you can be. But, we hasten to add here, that not all members of the congregation will care for music, and on the following page, we have a sample for these folks.

A SELECTION FOR THOSE WHO DISLIKE SINGING

Words by M. T. HEAD　　　　　　　　　　Music by IMA BETT FLAKEY

A SELECTION FOR THOSE WHO DISLIKE SINGING

Words by M. T. HEAD   Music by IMA BETT FLAKEY

A SELECTION FOR THOSE WHO DISLIKE SINGING

Words by M. T. HEAD   Music by IMA BETT FLAKEY

CHAPTER FIVE

In this chapter, we have some suggestions on how to improve your relationship with the pastor and the congregation. You need all the points you can get, and one way this can be helped, is always have the choir in the choir loft on time. It matters not whether they are ready, or even all there. If the service is to start at eleven o'clock, you should be ready to have them in the loft at exactly that time. On the following page is a simple suggestion that may be helpful.

"I KNOW I said you should get the choir here on time, Brother Rudy, but.........."

© Copyright 1984 by Light Headed Music Publishing Co., a division of Light Hearted Music Publishing Company, in *The Choir Director's Handbook?*

CHAPTER SIX

As noted in previous chapters, song or music selection should be done carefully, and should consider the individual choir member, or soloists or members of larger groups. Spare no effort in this area.

You will have some choir members who are good sight readers and some whose music reading is a sight. So, your music selection should take this into consideration. So you will know just what to look for, we have two illustrations below:

BROAD-MINDED MUSIC SAMPLE by Phar N. Wide

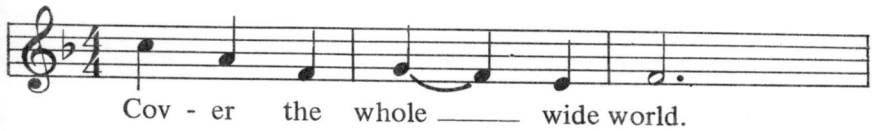

NARROW-
MINDED
MUSIC
SAMPLE
by
IMA VERA THIN

(Continued on next page)

mind - ed

song, It's

not as

wide as

some!

(There is no doubt that some of these samples will be thought of as only pertaining to the sample-minded person................. However, this is not so.)

CHAPTER SEVEN

As noted in the previous chapter, songs should be selected with the individual in mind who will be using this music. It should be perfectly clear to him or her, therefore, we have given you a sample of music that anyone should be able to see through. It is hoped that more music of this type will become available, because it is greatly needed.

MUSIC CLEAR ENOUGH FOR ANYONE TO SEE THROUGH

Open My Eyes

I. C. DeSONG   C. H. SCOTT

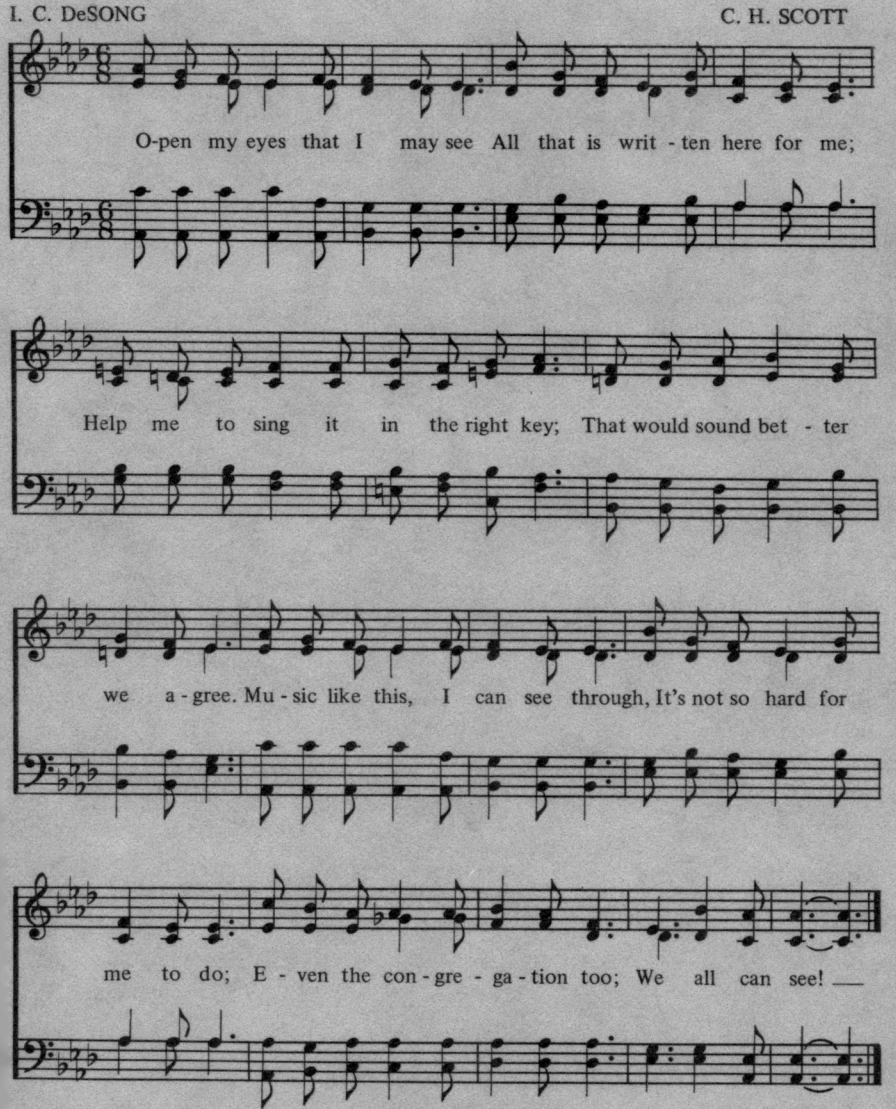

O-pen my eyes that I may see All that is writ-ten here for me; Help me to sing it in the right key; That would sound bet-ter we a-gree. Mu-sic like this, I can see through, It's not so hard for me to do; E-ven the con-gre-ga-tion too; We all can see!

New Lyrics © Copyright 1984 by Light Headed Music Publishing Co., a division of Light Hearted Music Publishing Company, in *The Choir Director's Handbook?*

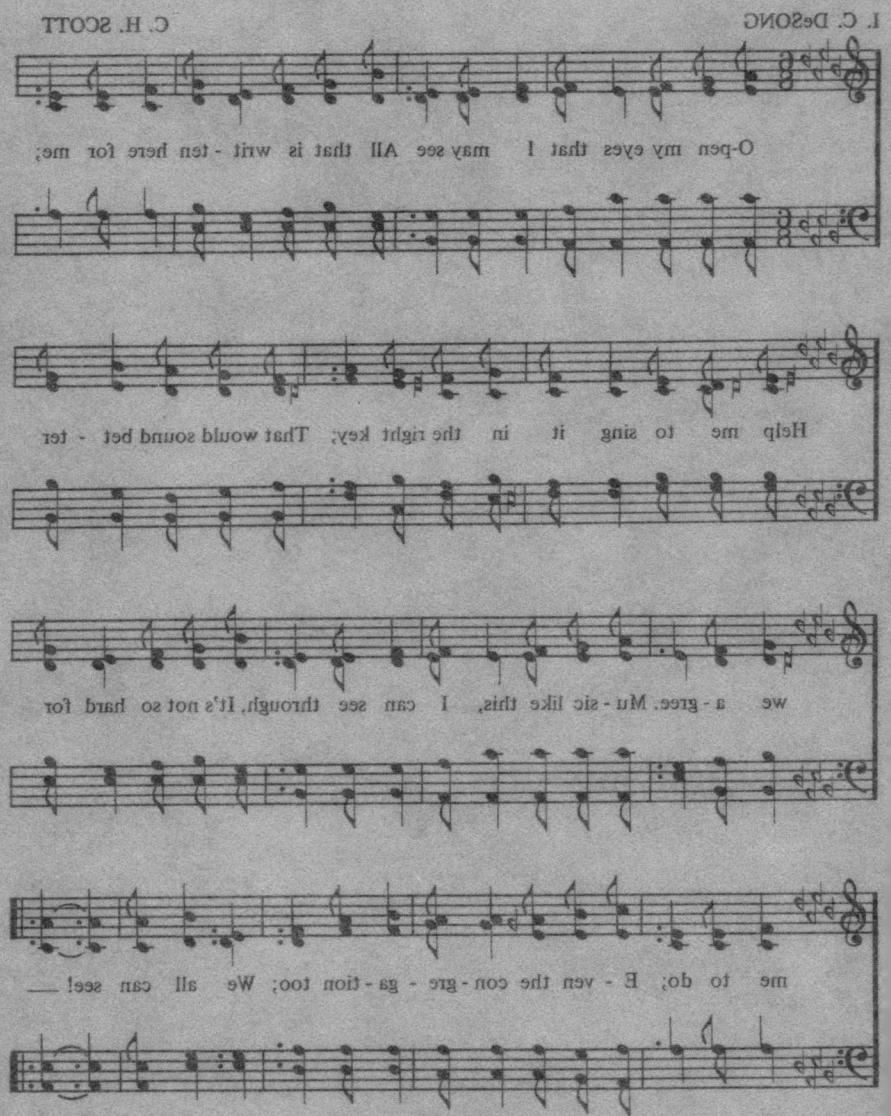

CHAPTER EIGHT

In addition to the individual, you may need music for larger groups. Often there is found a small choir slightly larger than one, which will mean you can call this group a Duet. Duet music is not always available, so we have included a selection here on the following page.

DUET MUSIC
O Perfect Love

DOROTHY B. GURNEY
JOSEPH BARNBY

1. O perfect Love, all human thought transcending,
2. O perfect Life, be thou their full assurance
3. Grant them the joy which brightens earthly sorrow;

Lowly we kneel in prayer before thy throne,
Of tender charity and steadfast faith,
Grant them the peace which calms all earthly strife,

That theirs may be the love which knows no ending,
Of patient hope and quiet brave endurance,
And to life's day the glorious unknown morrow

Whom thou for evermore dost join in one.
With child-like trust that fears no pain nor death;
That dawns upon eternal love and life. A-MEN.

During a period of great attendance promotion, you may have as many as three show up, and Trio Music will be necessary. It is hoped that this will not be too advanced for your group, but with help, success can be achieved. Just get them to give the following page a try!

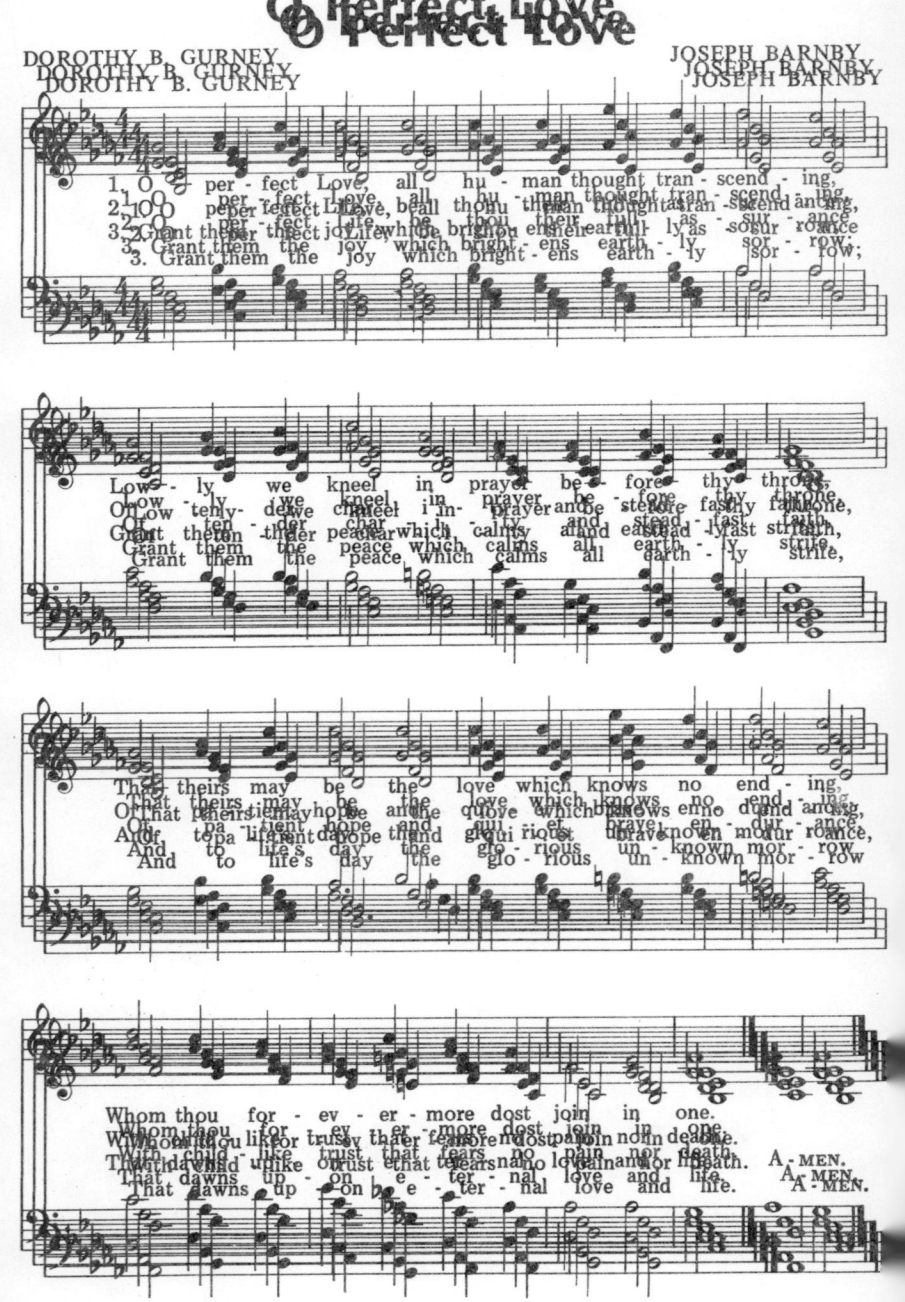

The Quartet is a very interesting experience, and is only slightly harder to try. All it takes is four, so do not let a fifth wheel intrude. The music will be more difficult to read since four people will be crowding around trying to see the music. Quartets should be used on the Fourth Sunday, July the 4th, and should only use music written in four-four time.

The following page is a good selection for the Quartet to use and should be a fine number.

QUARTET MUSIC
O Perfect Love

DOROTHY B. GURNEY
JOSEPH BARNBY

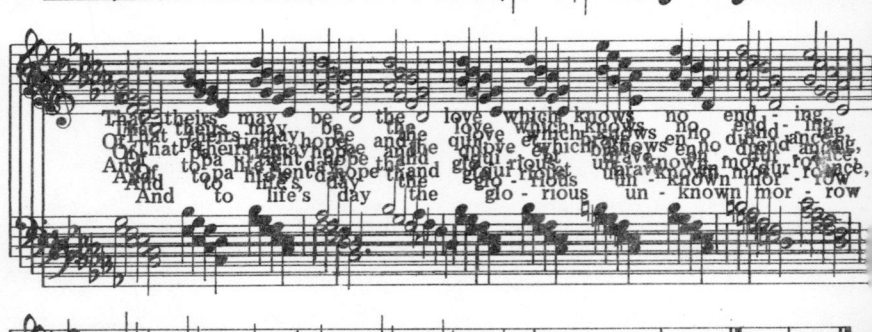
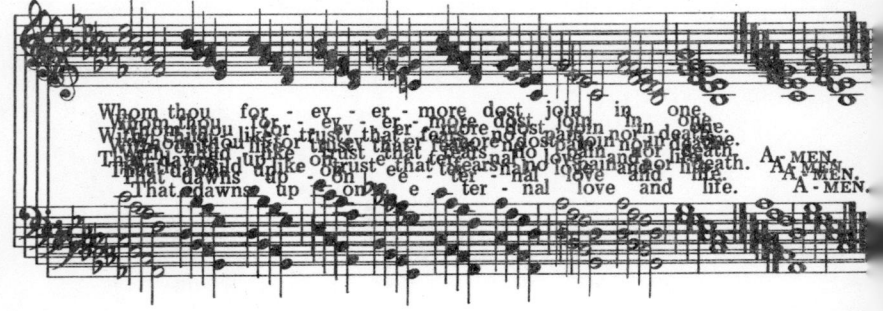

CHAPTER EIGHT

One of the problems in church services, is, they tend to be a little dry at times and some of the congregation may try to sleep through. Most pastors are ready to accept little innovations that will liven up the services. These can get out of hand, however, and we are almost reluctant to make suggestions in this area, but the following page will give you an idea. By now, you should have noticed we have two chapter "Eights" and was purely intentional. The first one seemed a bit short, and rather than compromise on quantity, we have included an additional chapter eight.

"I KNOW I said we should liven up the services, Brother Rudy, but............"

© Copyright 1984 by Light Headed Music Publishing Co., a division of Light Hearted Music Publishing Company, in *The Choir Director's Handbook?*

The following hymn was written and is here primarily to give some support to the members of the choir who depend or *LEAN* on other members of the choir. This may be in their quest for support on notes, words, or even when sleeping during the services where the choir is performing. It is just a subtle reminder that *LEANING* may be frowned upon. However, we have dealt with this problem in a more positive manner later on in the book. It will be found in the chapter which deals with arranging.

TOWER OF PISA HYMN

English Lyrics by ILENE A. LOTT
Chinese Translation by IRENE A. LOTT

Music by ANTHONY J. SHOWALTER
Music Arranged by I. M. ASKEW

Lyrics © Copyright 1984 by Light Headed Music Publishing Co., a division of Light Hearted Music ishing Company, in *The Choir Director's Handbook?*

CHAPTER NINE

After this bit of explanation, we want to jump right into a very difficult problem area that seems to apply to all choirs. This is the problem of monotones. I have never really considered it to be a great problem, but some folks do. I look at it this way. The Monotone actually is one of the better singers. True, his variety of notes is somewhat limited, but you must admit he is right in there on his pitch. Now, you must admit that all chords have one note or another as the basis for a chord to be formed, so why not form all the chords around your monotone and let him live it up? We have some music on the following page that should not prove too difficult for your organist or pianist. You may want to hum through it several times to familiarize yourself with the melody. Your monotone will probably know it before hand. If the key is wrong, it is not too hard to transpose.

Some monotones may sing a little flat, so this too should be taken into consideration. Try not to change this style, since any variation may be an improvement.

On a real positive line of thinking, you might want to have a choir made up entirely of "Monotones," although many of you may have one now as your regular choir. This group could be used during services that are held when a thunderstorm occurs, or during times when street construction is going on just outside the church building. Or, if your church is holding services on the runway of a large international airport during a rush period of landing and take-off activity. The choir would love it. But be persistent.

CHAPTER TEN

In this chapter, we will try to have a thorough discussion on Arrangements. This will begin as a seating arrangement, and then will quickly go into musical arrangements. This will be a challenging experience in both areas.

One of the simplest methods is to go into the choir room and say in a loud voice, "Be Seated!" Where each choir member sits can be used as a permanent arrangement, or you can be a little more creative. One method I like, which helps in mailing information to the choir members, is to line the choir up alphabetically by height. Some problem may arise in doing it this way, however, especially if all are the same height, or have names beginning with the same letter. For instance, "Shultz, Smith, Schantz, Smith, Scatzenberger, Smith, and Scazziano."

Arranging people is generally more difficult than arranging music. With people, it is placing people in the right spots. With arranging music, it is getting the spots in the right place.

One last thought on arranging people. It is wise to place some of your choir members where they can get a little sleep without too much worry of disturbing members of the congregation. This can be done by having several chairs or seats marked with a "D" for dozing. If there is a question from your pastor about this, tell him this is a reminder of which key the benediction is written in. These chairs should be behind the large chairs on the rostrum. If this is not possible, there should be arm rests on the chairs to prevent any excessive nodding during services.

Another method that can be used is heavy amounts of starch in the robes and stoles. This may not be possible if your choir does not have robes, because you can't just have the starch by itself. One director I knew used orthopedic collars, but this can be expensive and it is hard to convince your congregation that half the people in your choir have broken necks. But it is important to use your imagination in this problem area. But, if you do use the stiff collars, make mention that you have "A Chorus of a different Collar!"

Chapter Ten should be a fun chapter for everyone. We have placed notes in various positions on the page. Now, it is your turn to put them on the staff and make your own arrangement. Don't hurry.

PRACTICE PAGE FOR WRITING MUSIC OR ARRANGING

We warned you! Now we will see how well you have done. The following space should be used as a self-evaluation of your arranging or song writing ability:

Indicate with check marks which best describes your ability.

( ) Not too bad
( ) Not too good
( ) Mediocre
( ) Fair
( ) Inadequate
( ) Other (Please explain)

Other comments:

CHAPTER ELEVEN

One thing you should consider having in your church, is a pipe organ. Now, we realize that many small churches only have pianos, or electronic organs. However, Nothing gives the Choir Director the feeling of power, like a pipe organ. With just a little planning, I am sure you can enlist the help of your pastor in securing a pipe organ. So, let out all the stops and have a swell time in securing one.

One problem in getting help from your pastor in securing a pipe organ, he will want to appoint a committee to select it. You may have members on this committee who work for the *Kaywoodie Company,* and the *Yellow Bole Company,* and it may all end up as a pipe dream. But work at it. We have some helpful hints on the following page.

"I KNOW I said we needed a PIPE ORGAN, Brother Rudy, but…………"

© Copyright 1984 by Light Headed Music Publishing Co., a division of Light Hearted Music Publishing Company, in *The Choir Director's Handbook?*

CHAPTER TWELVE

We need to devote some time to one type of choir member who does not fall into any of the previous categories.

So, in this chapter, we will deal with the backward choir member. These generally sit on the back row, do not read music, or anything else for that matter. They require special handling and much wisdom. First, try directing from the back of the room. Granted, this may confuse some of your other choir members, but the backward ones will love it. Get special music for them. Provide them with mirrors. Give them lots of opportunities and many of them end up as back-up singers or musicians.

MUSIC FOR THE BACKWARD CHOIR MEMBER

CHAPTER THIRTEEN

Radio and T.V. production must be dealt with, because whether we like it or not, both mediums seem to be here to stay. For both of these, you should have your choir members of "medium" height. Now, one thing about T.V. If you close your eyes, it is almost as good as radio. However, it does create special problems.

Robes or the lack of them present a problem for T.V. If you have robes, you will not need to worry about this, but if not, you may want your choir to stand behind a very high choir rail, so that only the faces appear. This is also helpful, because the music is hidden and your T.V. audience will think the music is memorized. Radio is better in the fact that it eliminates all of the problems except singing well, and you can just use a recording and no one will notice the difference.

And, since we have mentioned recordings, this is an area where recordings and tapes are being used more and more in churches. These can work beautifully, and can really fool your congregations. Tell them you have an orchestra hidden in the baptistry and that is where the sound is coming from. And, too, if you really pour on the volume of these tapes, you can cover up a lot of mistakes in your choir.

CHAPTER FOURTEEN

We made chapter 13 rather short, because this number is somewhat unlucky.

In this chapter, we want to go into detail and make suggestions that will improve the quality of your directing.

You should try to balance your choir. This may be difficult to do, because some choir members will not want to be weighed. You should insist, however. Try to improve in every weigh.

Services should be kept short. Never use all three stanzas of *The Messiah* for a benediction.

SEVEN-FOLD AMEN

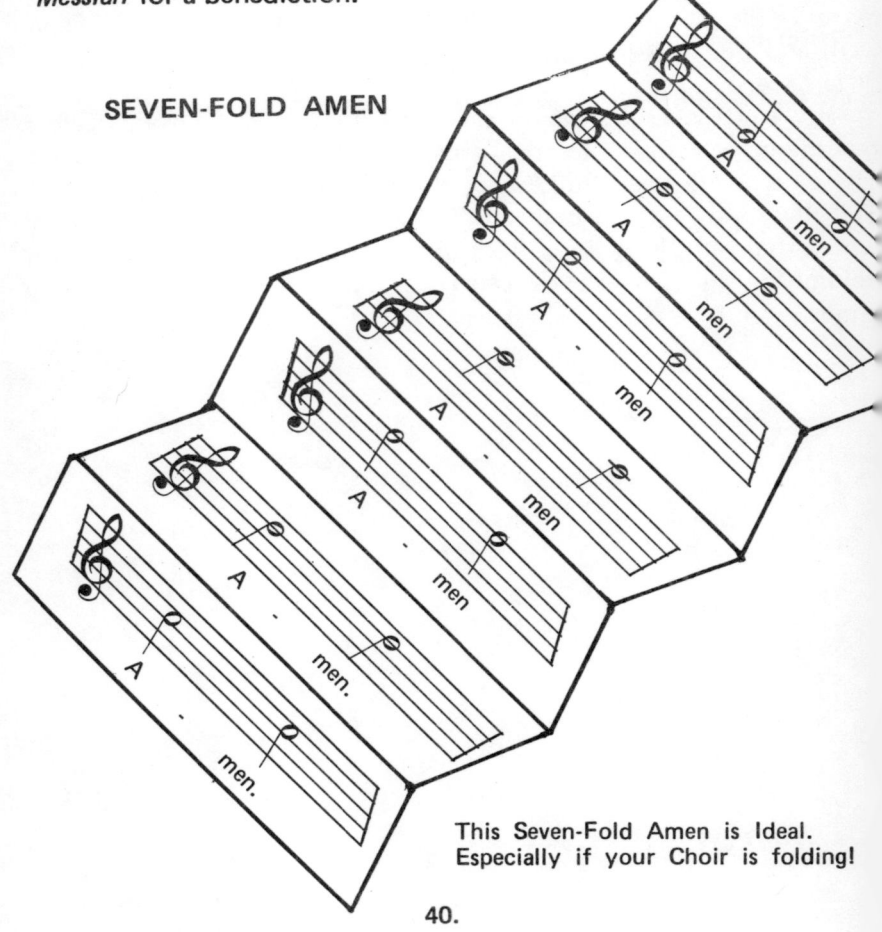

This Seven-Fold Amen is Ideal.
Especially if your Choir is folding!

CHAPTER FIFTEEN

Suggestions for Self-improvement:

_____
_____
_____
_____

CHAPTER SIXTEEN

Suggestions for: (Give your own choice)

_____
_____

CHAPTER SEVENTEEN

The following song is self-explaining. Please do it well!

GLOSSARY

BENEDICTION... A Movement by Early Patriots to avoid Mr. Arnold
CYMBAL ....The Opposite of Difficult
DESCANT............... Being Unable to Do Something. I descant do dat
FERMATA..............When you give Mother something—Fermata's Day
HARPSICHORD .... A rope used to tow a Harpsi with
HEPTAPHONOS................... A large, pig-like animal found in Africa
METRONOME......... A small person living in a large city or Metropolis
MIT BEGLEITUNG....... Singing while your Beagle Hound is Howling
POLONAISE.................................... A Salad Dressing Used in Poland
RUBATO ....Something to do when your foot is asleep
SARABAND ....An Orchestra directed by a girl named Sarah
SCHERZO.............. When everyone gets together to mend their shirts
TARANTELLA ....A Very Large Spider
SISTRUM... A place to store Water
TOCCATA ....A food served in Mexican Restaurants
WENIGA..A small German Sausage
WIEDERHOLUNG.............................A Doughnut with a bigger hole
TRUMPET .. A term used in card playing. Bridge or Rook or Pinochle
PINOCHLE ....A small boy whose nose grew long when he lied